CROWN ME!

CAPITAL POOL CHECKERS CLUB

813 S Street, NW
Washington, DC

Peggy Fleming

Photographs and conversations
PEGGY FLEMING

Text
Capital Pool Checkers Club Members

Foreword by MAURICE JACKSON
Edited by JENNIFER FLEMING

CROWN ME!

Capital Pool Checkers Club, 813 S Street, NW, Washington, DC
First Edition

Copyright 2010 © Peggy Fleming

ISBN 0-9676322-2-6
Library of Congress number 2010902894
1. Checkers – game
2. American Pool Checkers Association
3. Men's club
4. African American Men – Portraits
5. African American Men - Conversations
6. Washington DC
7. Baltimore, Maryland
8. United States – Social Life and Customs
9. Foreword - Maurice Jackson

Design by Alice Quatrochi, Jennifer Fleming, Rosemary Moak

City Game and three sisters press logo by Alice Quatrochi Designs

Photographs and conversations by Peggy Fleming

Printer: ColorCraft of Virginia, Inc. Sterling, VA 20164

Publisher: three sisters press, Washington, DC

For inquiries and to order the book: threesisterspress@13x.com

THREE
SISTERS
PRESS

Also by Peggy Fleming

IN HER PLACE: inner views and outer places. three sisters press 2000

SMALL TOWN IN THE BIG CITY: The shopkeepers and business community of Chevy Chase, Washington, DC, at the beginning of the 21st century. Co-author Joanne Zich. three sisters press 2005

CONTENTS

FOREWORD

MAURICE JACKSON

I am not much of a checkers player. I gravitated to billiards, then jazz and reading. But, I am a member of my version of the Checkers Club. The Listening Group was founded almost 20 years ago. We have a simple goal: to enjoy and preserve the music we call "Jazz." We meet once a month to listen to and discuss an aspect of the music, with good food and conversation. We discuss Bird and Monk, Ella and Sassy, Trane and Diz and the latest CDs. Like the Capital Pool Checkers Club, egos and professional identities are checked at the door. It does not matter whether one has a PhD or no D, a Mazeratti or a Mazda, a Buick or a Bronco. All that matters is what and how one contributes. Whether he's got "game." Our wives or significant others never complain about the Saturdays we meet. They know that we are doing something good for the individual and collective soul.

In Newport News, Virginia where I grew up, there were a few organized social clubs for Black men, but many rich and vibrant local gathering spots. MC's Pool Hall was one. At MC's, men gathered to shoot pool and shoot the breeze. Many of them could tell tales near equal to the greatest storyteller of all time, Satchel Page. At the pool hall, we listened until they ran us kids out, as men talked about the wars they had fought in, discrimination in the military, the military bands that they had played in and other stories of growing up in the Jim Crow South. Since my neighbors on both sides were longshoremen, when I came home from college for holidays or summers, I filled in on work gangs, at odd hours, or for some of the jobs that even Black longshoremen wouldn't take – like loading/unloading fish and tobacco. Later I dropped out of college and spent time as a "dock rigger" in the Newport News Shipbuilding and Dry Dock Company. We riggers had to be in the dock when the ships came into port to steer, tie and moor the ships in the dock. We often had long waits. Some men cooked. Others played chess or dominos, or talked. There was always a checkerboard at the local barber shop used by older gentlemen, whether they were getting haircuts or not. This pattern was not unique to Newport News or DC. Later, traveling to various parts of the world as an activist and writer, I often saw men bent over checkerboards in such places as Russia, Cuba, Grenada and the Dominican Republic.

Brotherhood and fellowship, so clearly reflected in the sense of community of the Capital Pool Checkers Club, has always existed among African-American men. The first Black male organization was founded by Prince Hall as the African Lodge Number One in Boston in 1775. When white Masons refused to allow Black men membership they simply formed their own society. Fraternal orders and benevolent societies followed. Men like W.E.B. Du Bois and Martin Luther King Jr. were among their members. Common to all of these was a sense of shared interest, experiences, mutual support and comradeship.

While Du Bois and Booker T. Washington had disagreements over the nature and pace of Black progress, they shared a belief on the collective purpose of Black men. Washington and his supporters believed that "of deeper significance if possible, than equality before the law…is equality of industry…he who earns his bread by sweat of his brow is, in our teachings, as much entitled to respect and honor as he who rules an empire and enjoys with him an equality of fraternity, friendship and recognition." Du Bois wrote two chapters in his immortal *Souls of Black Folk*, often called "The Black Bible," about the special role he felt that African-American men must play in society.

Over the century since these sentiments were expressed, much has changed. The partial breakdown of class distinctions within the Black community is one of the most profound. Like the Listening Group, when the Capital Pool Checkers Club members meet, distinctions based on income or education go out the window. The big question is, can you play and are you helping to pass on the legacy of the game?

The men of the Capital Pool Checkers Club come from all walks of life. They are cab drivers and physicists, barbers, university professors and musicians, landscapers and artists. From their stories it is clear that they are "men of distinction." Mary Church Terrell, the founder of the National Association of Colored Women and who played a major role in integrating Washington, DC, put it simply in 1898, "And so lifting as we climb, onward and upward we go, struggling and striving, and hoping that the buds and blossoms of our desires will burst into glorious fruition ere long."

In this book, Peggy Fleming has captured the essence of what good men do when they do good things together. Of men who have lifted as they have climbed.

Maurice Jackson is Associate Professor of History and African American Studies and Affiliated Professor of Music at Georgetown University. He is author of the critically acclaimed book, Let This Voice be Heard: Anthony Benezet, Father of Atlantic Abolitionism *(2009). He is co-editor with Jacqueline Bacon of* African Americans and the Haitian Revolution: Select Articles and Historical Documents, *(2010). He is a 2009 inductee into the Washington, DC, Hall of Fame and at work on a social, political and cultural history of African Americans in Washington, DC from the 1700's until the present.*

Essay

PEGGY FLEMING

Like many other rewards in my life, my introduction to the Capital Pool Checkers Club in my hometown, Washington, DC, was accidental. For years I'd been working on a photography project about people who live in Washington. A friend, Pernell Lee, told me about his checkers club and brought me around to introduce me to its president, Tal Roberts. As Tal and I talked, members arrived and I watched and listened. This was too good a photography opportunity to pass up: I offered to make portraits of the members, then decided to interview them about their game and about their lives in Washington – how they got here if they weren't natives and how they fared during the city's turbulent years of inspiration and of despair.

The club looks like what you might imagine: three tables set with six checkerboards in the center of the room. Oldies but goodies soul music playing, punctuated by the staccatos of the checkers as they are moved and the triumphant declarations, "Put a hat on it" or "Crown Me." Cell phones ringing, the vending machine humming, the refrigerator opening and closing, corn popping. Adorning one wall are hundreds of snapshots of current and former members. Trophies reign high up on a shelf. Sofas and chairs, worn with use. The men sit, stand, watch and play, kibitzing. The atmosphere is friendly but the game is serious and competitive.

The members of the Capital Pool Checkers Club have gathered at 9th and S Streets, NW, in Washington since 1985. The club is an affiliate of the American Pool Checkers Association. The game played by the members is called Spanish pool checkers. Straight checkers is what most of us know and played. Spanish pool checkers is more complicated and involves different rules for jumping and moving. According to the association, Spanish pool has been played, predominately by Blacks, throughout the United States. "Straight checkers was too slow and not exciting in moving nor jumping so it was not as appealing," the association says. The APCA holds national and regional tournaments. While many of the members of the Checkers Club compete in the tournaments – and often win – some come to the club just to relax in the camaraderie.

The men know one another by their "handles," their "checker names." "Sometimes you know people by their nickname and don't know their real name," Tal said. "We had one called E. C. Taylor, and his name was E.C. We never knew what his real name was because his real name was Ecclesiastes. And there were a lot of people couldn't pronounce it. And nobody could spell it."

In this book you will meet *The Shark, Chicago, The Stealer, Boy Wonder, The Weasel, Johnnie Cool, The Master of Disaster* and *The Hawk,* among others.

I started photographing and interviewing the members on Saturday afternoons in January 2007. Each conversation lasted about an hour. I transcribed the interviews and edited them, but I didn't change them; I tried to preserve the fragmented, colloquial conversational way we talk. What comes through, I hope, is the fraternal affection derived from a shared interest in checkers, and these honorable citizens' narrative memories of their lives and their city's life over the past half-century.

Most of the men are about my age, and, like me, most came to Washington in the 1950s for education and job opportunities. I was born in 1937, in California, the first daughter of an Italian mother and Irish father. When I graduated from college, my father gave me an airplane ticket to Washington, a one-night hotel reservation and one hundred dollars. It was August of 1959. My first job was as a secretary in Senator John F. Kennedy's office. I worked for Kennedy for four years – in the Senate, during his presidential campaign, and in the White House, always on civil rights issues.

Like these checkers players, I remember the historic moments: marching on August 28, 1963 and being at the foot of the Lincoln Memorial for the "I Have A Dream Speech"; the city erupting in flames in 1968. Here I raised my children in the '70s and here, on a bitterly cold but joyous day, Janary 20, 2009, I attended the Inauguration of Barack Obama. Since the first night I arrived, I have, like many of these men, watched the city struggle and grow and shift.

I am grateful for the hospitality shown me by the men of the Checkers Club. As player Tony Simuel said about Obama, "He really means to bring people together. That's how we solve problems that we have in the world, to have people working together. Just like you. If nobody gave you an interview, it's useless. So you come, and everybody work together to give a good interview."

CROWN ME! is 24 portraits. In the two pages that follow each player is his story of how he got hooked by the game, how the game influences his life and some information about his life. The recorded tapes, transcripts and photographs have been donated to the American Folklife Center at the Library of Congress in Washington and the Kiplinger Research Library, Historical Society of Washington at 801 K Street NW at Mount Vernon Square, Washington DC.

"I used to play all day and every night," says the former cab driver George Glenn. "I limit myself now. I may play three or four times a month, but I don't play no more than four or five days in succession. I come here every day, unless I'm out of town or sick or something. This is my second home."

I'm glad I found George Glenn at home. It was a wonderful welcome. I feel crowned.

CROWN ME!

PORTRAITS AND CONVERSATIONS

TALMADGE ROBERTS

OZARK, ALABAMA (1931)

"I give close shaves. I became so skillful at what I was doing that I could cut people and they didn't even bleed. They didn't even know they were cut. So I performed surgery on them."

The Razor

Talmadge Roberts, 79
CAB DRIVER, CHEMIST, STOCKBROKER, BUSINESS OWNER

I grew up in Alabama on a farm. Our house was maybe two or three miles from any other house. We lived at the end of the road, at the end of everything. We had a big family. We had no television, no electric lights, no running water. So what our parents did to keep us entertained, they made a checkerboard. A checkerboard was made simply from taking a piece of cardboard, blocking 'em off, and taking checkers – which were bottle tops, one up, one down – and let us play.

I didn't show a great interest in school. When I first started I was considered slow: could not count, definitely couldn't read. To be a good checkers player I had to be able to count. When you do all that intricate jumping sometimes you think you got it right, but you got it wrong. Oftentimes when I made all these jumps, I came up on the losing end. One plus one, two; one plus two equals three. That's how I learned how to count.

My grandmother used to take us around to see her children. I think it would take us two or three days to go from Ozark, Alabama to Pittsburgh, Pennsylvania. It was exciting to me to ride on the train. The wheels were taller than we were. And let me tell you, what excited me so much on the train, it looked like our train was standing still when the train next to us was moving, and of course the steam would come out *whoosh-ah*.

My parents migrated to Pennsylvania. I think I was in the 7th grade. After graduating high school, I went to the service. My whole purpose of going to the service was I needed a job and the service represented a job. Employment. During the service, the Korean conflict broke out. So when I got ready to get out of the service, I was going back to Pennsylvania to work in the steel mill. Bethlehem Steel. I had not intended to go to school. I didn't think I could afford it. I didn't think I had any intelligence for it.

My uncle invited me to come to Washington and stay with him until I got myself situated. My uncle was a chauffeur for Henry B. Steagall, a Representative from Alabama (1915-1943). In Washington everything was exciting: streetcars, traffic lights, grocery stores, people living next door to you, people up at twelve and one o'clock at night. He introduced me to Howard University. I had an educational benefit from being a Korean War Veteran. I was accepted on the provision that I complete a refresher course. I had been out of school for a while, so they didn't know whether I had the determination to really hit the books. I finished those classes and finished the first year with M-A-G-N-A C-U-M L-A-U-D-E. Shocked the daylights out of me. So I majored in chemistry, minored in biology and then was accepted in medical school. I spent a year in medical school. I drove a cab, I guess just about the entire time I was in Howard, to supplement my income. My income was ninety dollars a month. Took care of food, clothing, expenses. Everything I needed. I got a job as a chemist with the Food and Drug Administration. Suddenly my life just opened up. Life wasn't quite so hard. I ended up being a stockbroker and Assistant Vice President at Paine Webber. So a lot of good things happened to me. I decided I maybe wasn't quite as dumb as people thought.

I pretty much owe my life to the game of checkers. Now I compete on a national level. Our players are primarily from the United States. From time to time we have visitors from South America and Russia.

There are five competition levels: *Blue Ribbon* is the first level, *Gold Bar* is the second level of accomplishment, *Junior Master* is mid level, *Master* is fourth level and *Top Master* is fifth level. I compete on the third level for the past four years. I hope to complete that this year and win the tournament and move on to the next level.

I've been the president of the club for 15 years. We're a community-based organization that plays checkers. We help out individual members, in case they are sickly. From time to time, our members reach hard times. One of our members is now incarcerated, been so for four years. We try to visit and correspond with him on a regular basis. At Christmas, we try to provide some toys for the children.

Our saying is *"Do good by doing good."*

JOHN CURTIS

BALTIMORE, MARYLAND (1940)

"When you hit deep water and you can't swim, you're in trouble. You better know where you're going. If you don't, I'll get you. You see, sharks are cold, cold-blooded animals."

The Shark

John Curtis, 70
INSURANCE AGENT, BUSINESS OWNER, SOUTHERN COOK

I was playing out near my business, just playing a friendly game with some of the local guys, and one of my students, who was a lieutenant in the police force, she said her father belongs to a checkers club. And like all men, you want to rule and conquer. I came down here.

They brought me to a rude awakening and a stark reality that I was far from the best. What hooked me then was the guy defeated me, and I don't care if I'm playing tiddlywinks, I don't want to get beat. I have a thing about "Me getting beat? Me? Of course not." I was winning out there on the sidewalk and the guys just passed me around and were laughing. I found out how much I didn't know. I was so embarrassed. I was so disgusted with myself. I didn't realize I was just so low on the totem pole.

I took my lumps on the chin. I was determined I was going to elevate myself. I came back in after about two to three weeks of getting over myself. I came back nice and humble, this time. Last time, when I first came in, I was proud and sticking my chest out, all full of braggadocio, but when I left, I was eating humble pie. So that started my quest of climbing up the checker ladder of success.

An old man told me one time, he said, "Son, if you're going to learn how to play checkers, learn how to draw a game." I said, "I don't want to draw no game." And he said, "Yeah, but a draw is better than a loss. You have to learn how to draw." So there's an art to learning how to draw a game. It's also frustrating too.

One of the main points you have to employ when you play checkers is patience, and kindness. You have to be patient. I think I beat Freddie Owens maybe once or twice out of maybe 300 games. It wasn't because I was so good. Freddie just got tired of playing. But Freddie plays people from all over the United States. They come from all over just to beat him and play him. He just beats them. Freddie's been playing since he was like 14 or 15 years old and he was a top player when he was 19. And he's in his 60s.

The American Psychiatric Society says that if you can employ any kind of a board game you wouldn't have to worry about Alzheimer's. It delays or defrays Alzheimer's. In checkers you have a maximum of three million moves. That's a lot of moves. That's a lot of scenarios. That's a lot of combinations. That's a lot of traps. Can you imagine how much electrical firing is going on in your brain to try to keep up with that? Mental calisthenics! It keeps you young.

I spent 27 years as an insurance agent and I was one of the top salesmen in the entire country. I went from there to the cosmetology school, South Capital Beauty Academy, in Washington DC. I bought the school with my savings. When I had my own cosmetology school I would invite the guys up to my school and we'd get a lot of food. I come from Virginia. So actually what I did was a lot of cooking. And they loved my cooking, like they do today. If you ask any of them about my fish, they tell you absolutely "Voila." I can do more with a crab than the Chesapeake Bay. I could cook anything – ground hog, coon, possum, squirrel, rabbit, deer, bear, geese, duck, pheasants – you name it, I can cook it. If it got fur or feathers or scales, I can cook it. I'm a good 'ole Southern boy. Not one of those Italian this and French that. As far as good Southern cooking, I can make a piece of wood taste good.

In the summer, I sell fish sandwiches, chicken sandwiches and crabs. I do real good with it. Most of which, I donate to the club. I'm a people person really and because of my gregarious personality it really helps my sales. So it's good. I'm a typical Virgo – a workaholic.

I went to Baltimore, because my mother was sick. I had to make a choice, the school or my Mom? There was no choice. Easy choice. She's the originator and I'm just the imitator, and you know I'm going to look out for her. I got little duplicators and they even have little assimilators and we all look out for Moms.

THOMAS FLETCHER

SANTIAGO, CUBA (1933)

"I play cold-blooded position. I play to win. I find that to be one of my weaknesses. I don't play to draw. When somebody sits in front of me, I play to win. And sometimes I lost games trying to win a draw."

Hard Fletch

Thomas Fletcher, 77
CAB DRIVER, BUSINESS OWNER, MAINTENANCE

When I moved down here I decided to find a place where the guys were playing checkers, because I like to watch the game also. I came from New York and I been playing up there in New York. Originally I played for the Brooklyn Elite Club in New York. I went to the tournament in Winston Salem in '78. Through John Curtis, I was able to find out that they had a club in DC. So I was invited and I came over. I was somewhat enjoying the atmosphere, so my few visits over they asked me if I wanted to join, so I did. It's a place I can come and relax myself. Get away from the frustration of all the negative stuff.

I play checkers based on my position. Some people, they look for what they call shots, but I usually play position. Shots are OK if you can catch a person, but you can't really rely on that, because if you play an opponent that is equal caliber like you, they may see what you saw and they may evade that and be in a better position and defeat you. So I just eliminate that and play the cold-blooded position. If the shot comes up in the position, then it's OK. But other than that I just play position. I try to play as strong as possible to defeat the opponent.

Memory is very demanding in this game. You have to have a very good memory and you have to have good focus and an analytical mind. I know guys who could go back 25 years on games that they played, you know, and even some moves that was made, and they could go back and tell you the guy who they played it with. I'm not that good. My memory is somewhat shot. I take ginkgo biloba and ginseng and essential fatty acids to boost the brain and Vitamin B12 and bee pollen. So I'm trying to keep my physical condition in shape. Because, you know, this game requires a lot of mental energy and if you're not well focused, then your game would not be.

I was born in Santiago, Cuba. I really don't have too much memory of Cuba. I grew up in Panama. I came there when I was small. I was playing checkers when I was about 10 years old. We used to play with soda tops and things like that and the small board. Kids were playing the soda tops and the grownups were playing on the big board, the 40 man, 20-20 each. The 40 man game is played different from the small board. On the small board you jump from your own choice. On the big board you have to jump the most pieces. That's the basic international rule. I play both boards. I play big and I play small.

I originally grew up playing the big board and I couldn't find any body, any player, any place, that they were playing the big board. So when I went into the park in New York, I saw the guys playing the small board, so I had to go back to the small board and play that because there was no big board at Tompkins Park in Brooklyn, New York.

I used to work at the hospital in the beginning. Then I bought me a cab and started to drive that on the side. I wanted to get me a house and things like that for my family. In Brooklyn, New York. After that I bought me a truck, went into the trucking business doing hauling and moving and cleaning out basements. From that I open up a store, a clothing store, and after that I went and bought me a delicatessen. That lasted for about six, seven years, and then I went out of business because the neighborhood got so bad. So I just decided, I went and got me a job working for the city of New York, the housing authority. I retired maintenance, housing repairman.

I was moving to Georgia, but my son, living in Maryland, he asked me, "Why you want to go so far? You could stay here. This way you're closer to your family." So I said, "Well, it makes sense, you know." I wound up in Maryland in '99.

OLIVER GRIFFIN

NATCHEZ, MISSISSIPPI (1934)

"I like thinking that when I get up from the table, no one can tell whether I won or lost. I don't brag about winning and I don't get mad if I lose."

The Stealer

OLIVER GRIFFIN, 76
MATHEMATICIAN

I lived in Baltimore and I had a season ticket to the Baltimore Colts. I went by a friend of mine's house after the game and we sat around and had a few drinks and one guy who was there said, "Can anybody here play checkers?" and a friend of mine that worked where I worked at said, "Yes, I can play." So we all set up a match the next week and when they did I looked at the interested group. All the ladies were around and they were just *oohing* and *aahing* and I said, "This is the game I think I need to play." My interest was piqued.

I used to take a checkerboard around in my trunk, a board that was on a tray, a dinner tray. I set up near shopping centers. We didn't have the big malls at that time, just small shopping centers. I just take two chairs, two folding chairs, and the tray with the checkerboard and the checkers. People used to come by, see you playing and they wanted to make a dollar or two off you. They think they see a rookie out there, might want to bet a dollar or two. I never progressed to big money. Just one dollar or two.

I was surprised the first time I came here because I couldn't win a game. And that's what you call like a comeuppance. I had my comeuppance, but I was still infatuated. So they tell me, "Oh, you play good." I knew better, but they wanted me to come back, so they didn't discourage me. Some people here you know you're better than, but you don't want to beat them because you don't want to discourage them 'cuz no one discouraged me. I will always say, "Do you mind if I show you something?" And if they say OK, I show them. A good checker player always wants to learn.

If you just lost a game, we don't want to know why you did and whatever reason you had. You lost. I'm about to show you how to win. You know. How to draw. First, you want a draw because you don't want a loss at all costs, at any cost. And next you want to be able to win the game. I was reading the back of this old checkerboard that folds, which costs a dollar, dollar and a half. And it says, "Play people who are better than you whenever possible." So whenever possible I still do.

I was a mathematician. I came in the Army, 1956, Aberdeen, Maryland. Proving Grounds. Ballistic Research Lab. I was a research analyst, Research and Weapons Systems. Then I became a statistical engineer when I went to New Jersey. When I came down here I was a mathematical statistician at the Pentagon. So they had me doing some budget analysis work. A very rewarding professional life.

I remember when I started with the budget, a lady asked me, "Would you rather be a mathematician or a budget analyst?" And the thing is, it depends on where you are. If you are around people that deal with a lot of money, you want to be a budget analyst. If you are around people who just want to look upon you as being sort of capable of doing something, then you want to be a mathematician. Because everybody remembers what they did when they were in school and whether math was easy for them or hard. I was talking to this guy. He said, "What in the world made you ever want to become a mathematician?" So to me that means some respect, you know. Little thing.

We have a national tournament every year. I won a trophy, fifth place, in Memphis, in 2007 and I won a trophy, third place, in Columbus, Ohio, in 2006. I won the DC championship here in 2003, which included people of higher rank. When I won a trophy nationally, that was my crowning glory.

There is some reluctance to play Freddie, because a lot of people just don't want to lose. He is one of the best, in the United States, in the world. Anybody can ask anybody. One thing about Freddie, I've never seen him refuse to play anybody. He'll play a teenager, I mean a little teenager. And I found out when I asked him to play he didn't say, "Well I'll play you this many games." He just played until I told him, "I'm going to play you two more games and that's it." He's such a good sport. I mean, he's a wonderful guy. This is what makes it a good club. People cooperate.

GEORGE GLENN

WHITMIRE, SOUTH CAROLINA (1931)

"If anybody wants to find me, like my doctor, they all know where I'm at. They call here."

House Man

GEORGE GLENN, 79
CAB DRIVER, TEAMSTERS UNION-LOCAL 82, LANDSCAPER

I used to play all day and every night. I started having headaches. I had to cut back on it to find out what was going on. I talked to the doctor and he said the strain. I limit myself now. I may play three or four times a month, but I don't play no more than four or five days in succession. I come here every day, unless I'm out of town or sick or something. This is my second home.

I play checkers when I was a little boy. But I come into this club seven years ago. I had a club down at 4th and N Street Northwest. It wasn't nothing but policemen, firemen, and postal office workers. Everybody retired. But they didn't play no checkers, you know, and I play checkers. Well they sit around and drink, played cards but didn't play checkers. I wanted to play checkers. So I stayed down there 'til the club fold up, then I come here. We start here on Friday night and we go to ten o'clock in the morning. Too much you know. That take a toll on anybody, you know. At my age, I can't do it.

I had to limit myself from doing things. I do very little of anything now. Go to hospital two or three times a week; I have classes that I go to. Korea, post, you know, when you go and talk about things that happened, that you went through. Korea Veterans. We talk to try to help us. Veterans of Foreign Wars.

I'd been working on 14th Street that night and the news came on that they shot Martin Luther King. I got up and went to the liquor store and got a pint of gin. I told my old lady that before I could get back from the liquor store they started burning up everything. The liquor store owner, he ran out and said, "You all help yourself. I'm going." I could see 14th Street bubbling up fire. I went on back and me and my girlfriend we went on into Maryland. But we didn't know what was going to happen. So close when it happened and I was in the area. I didn't see anything like that in the Army like I seen during that time. I could start up on 13th Street Northwest and see all over, the fire. I was scared. Just coming out of the Army too.

First time I come here was 1949. I was 16 years old. I was living at 2024 G Street Northwest, and I was working at a job at 13th and E, O'Donnell's Sea Grill. I used to come behind the White House to go to work, to go to my job, and this is where it happened. They tried to assassinate Truman.

And I went back South to get in the Army. I was too young, and finally I got in at the right age. I went in service in South Carolina. I got out of service, in 1958. Been here ever since. I was young, you know, but it was an experience, 'cuz coming from the country, you know, it is always coming to a city like this, you know, an experience, but I'd never been no place until I was in the service.

I drove a long time, cab for 30 years and 15 years in Army. Started in '62. I was driving when President got killed. I was driving then. He got assassinated. I was downtown. I retired from my job the same night. I was working for the Teamsters Union Local 82. I resigned the same night. The day President Kennedy got killed.

I had a lot of cab drivers in my company where I drove cab at Globe Cab. And two or three guys here was in the company and finally they talked me into it. I don't play nothing but checkers. I never did learn how to play chess. I have a lot of friends in here. I have a lot of friends I've known for years. We've all known each other, doing the same thing every day. I stopped driving cabs in 1985. I retired and was in business for myself, for a long time, a landscaper. I used to have a garden every year since I retired and do a little fishing and gardening. But I don't do that now that I have the pacemaker put in. So I guess that's my life story.

John Henry Self

GREENWOOD, SOUTH CAROLINA (1936)

"Camaraderie. It's camaraderie. There's a chance to come and talk. You can talk politics, of which none of us knows anything about."

The Steel Driving Man

That's probably no one, no one in the Checkers Club that's been playing any longer than I. I started playing checkers when I was about seven or eight years old, standing around in Greenwood and watching the elder men play. If no other elder person was there, they would show you. Then as we got better, a young man about eight or nine years old would beat somebody that's 30 years old. And the older men would say, "You let that kid beat you?" They would get angry and say, "No. You can't play." But I learned.

I learned, not with the boards like we have here, all fancy boards, all fancy checkers. We used to use the soda tops and you turn yours down and I turn mine up. That was an advantage there. Sometimes you didn't have 12. Sometimes you might be playing with 20, because every time you jump one, you wouldn't be looking and he put another one back on the board.

I don't have a rank because I've never been to a tournament and I'm not exactly up on titles. Some people carry these titles, can't play squat. You see what I'm saying? They like to go into the tournament and say, "What group did you play?" "I play in Blue Ribbon or Gold Bar or Master." Come on. Give me a break. I beat you and I ain't in no bar. So titles? I'm not... If I can beat a man, I can beat him. I don't care what title he is. It's not difficult. Checkers is not that heavy.

The House Man is from Greenwood. Plus we served in the military together in Germany. He's a little bit older than I am. I knew him when I was going to high school. He went back in the military. Then we hooked up again in the military and then our paths crossed when he was driving cab and then our paths crossed again in 1990 here at the Checkers Club. Every 20 years we meet.

I came to Washington because I wanted to better my conditions as far as work was concerned. I wasn't that impressed. I had served in the military and I had served in Germany, so I wasn't exactly a wide-eyed youngster at 27 years of age. First impression was to find a job, and a good paying job. First job I had, I worked for Pepsi-Cola. I worked there for a year and a half and then I moved on to Wonder Bread, Teamsters 118. You could almost find a job just walking down the street then. And it was much easier if you knew somebody within that industry who could recommend you. In those times, if you had somebody who had been on the job for eight or nine years, and they recommended you, they would most likely take you. If you went in and applied by an application, they would say, "No, we don't have anything." But if somebody brought you, they say, "OK. He OK 'cuz Joe's OK." I don't know if that was a good idea, but I certainly took advantage of it.

I worked for Wonder Bread for 32 years. When I first went there you got the smell and then when people pass by they say, "Do you smell the bread?" "Nope. I don't smell a thing." Only time I could smell it was when it was burning. And everybody ought to be able to smell burnt bread, shouldn't they?

My friend who is deceased started up here and he would find these people to play and he would always, "Man, I met this guy, come on let's go play." I guess you see all these pictures and photographs of them up here. This little building used to be jam packed with checker players. Lot of 'em from South Carolina, North Carolina. They had migrated up here. We play other checker clubs from down there.

In fact, last week, I think it was last week or week before last, they had a group up here from North Carolina and, no, it was two weeks ago, and then last week they had a young man came from New York down to play, one of the top notch players. To play Kim. Kim's pretty good. He's new here but he's been playing. He's young though.

KIM WILLIAMS

PORTSMOUTH, VIRGINIA (1963)

"I like the learning aspect of the game. Checkers is a good game for study. I like to study. I like to learn. So I call myself the teacher."

The Teacher

KIM WILLIAMS, 47
PROPERTY MANAGEMENT

It was in a corner store in the neighborhood. I saw some older guys playing and I suspected they were playing checkers but I wasn't sure, so I stopped in and watched them play. At the time I was not aware of the depth of the game. Checkers is one of those games that outwardly seems simplistic. There're all kinds of computer programs and all kinds of books on the game of checkers.

Most of the theoreticians on the game are Russians, but if you ever get into checker programs, the web or various writers of the checker program, you see the depth of the game. There's one game that I've been playing for about five years called *Crossing*. And after five years of studying this game, I am still discovering different moves in this particular game. Most people would not be aware of it. Napoleon was an avid checker player and a lot of the hieroglyphics, Egyptian, had checkerboards on 'em. It's an enormously popular game internationally, but it's not as popular in the United States. It is a very engaging, captivating game.

Last year I won the national championship in Gold Bar Division. I won first place in national championship last year, so I've been promoted to Junior Master. I have a trainer by name of Al Harrison, out of Wilmington, North Carolina, and he's a good checker player. He's a Top Master checker player, and I think his commitment is to doing the best, but then, see I have a philosophical approach to life. I think being successful is to maximize on your potential. And I think a person that maximizes on their potential in playing checkers is a success. I take a philosophical approach to what makes a good checker player, because not everybody is at the same level in learning. Capabilities. I see it as maximizing on your potential, which will make you a good checker player at your level.

The thing that's fascinating is that most checkers players have alter egos and they name their alter egos. And sometimes their alter egos have a first and last name, which makes it interesting. So the personality is another thing that draws you to the game because it's not just moving checkers on the board, but it's a matter of fellowship with the people. So the fellowship, coupled with how engaging the game is.

Actually I played the Russians, picked up in a side game. There are no Russians to my knowledge who went to the national tournament. There was one Russian analyst who was just observing different games. Usually when the Russians show up they tend to dominate, because it's more of a cultural thing for them. It's imbedded in their culture. There's a Russian by the name of Jake Kacher who wrote an article on me on the tournament in 2007, predicting that I was a future star. I feel I'm a Top Master player. I believe I can go to the top.

This guy here is considered one of the best players in the country. That's Freddie.

Good shot. Good shot. Good shot brother.

GABE CURTIS BROTHERS

EDENTON, NORTH CAROLINA (1952)

"I dream checkers. Plenty of times my wife wakes me up. She said sometimes I be telling people, 'Your move' or 'I'm going to take that man.'"

Brothers

GABE CURTIS BROTHERS, 58
NAVY YARD, DRIVER

I started many years ago, watching my father, and people on the street. They had this old checkerboard, with soda tops. Slammin' down, talkin' trash, you know. I used to sit around and watch them. I just watched 'em for such a long time, I sort of picked up on it. Ever since then I fell in love with it. I start playing at age seven or eight. I started off playing *Give Away* with my sisters and brothers. But that was nothing. Then I started playing straight checkers, like you can't move backward, and then from there I moved up to Spanish pool, which is what professionals play. Spanish pool.

I worked for the Department of Navy in the Navy Yard for 31 years and four months. Everyday, I make a phone call, see somebody be down here playing, come down here. I play checkers every day. My wife says I'm addicted to this game. Addicted to this checkers. You can play this game for hours. Hours at a time. Time go by so fast you don't realize. Two people could play for at least 15 hours, without stopping. Well, to go to the bathroom of course. Sometime you come, start playing like two o'clock and play all day long, all through the night, next day. An addiction. An addiction.

As a matter of fact, I thought I was the best player in Washington DC when I first got here. I thought I was the best player there was until I found this club at 9th and S. I happened to come in here one day, play some guys and that's when the competition picked up. I didn't realize these guys could play it as well as they could. Most people that play checkers are good mathematicians, because they can see things long ways away. You don't look one or two moves ahead; you know about 12 moves ahead. I play some of the best players in here. If you play stronger players, then your chances are you'll be much, much stronger.

Chess is a really good game, but checkers is about the same. What you probably don't know about checkers, there are over 100,000 different moves. A whole lot of people don't realize that. I know quite a few of them. You have to do that, if you play professional. Of course your opponent knows a whole lot of moves as well. So you got to go on defense, offense, a strategy.

I play for the strength. I move and watch my opponent move. I'm aggressive. I try to play aggressive, make the other person make certain moves and when they do that, I go in for the kill. I go in for the kill. I take all their men. This game is like the hunter and the hunted. Kill or be killed. And I don't like draws. I don't like draws. I like to win. Try to go for the kill, at all times. I always try to dominate your opponent.

Many years ago, they used to play this game for people's lives. People's lives. People actually used to get killed over checkers. Ulysses started it I heard. A man jump another man, they kills him. So this game originate a long, long, long time ago.

I want to be the top player in the United States. Beat Freddie, Calvin Monroe, which won the tournament, Top Master Division. He's the top player. I want to beat him. That is my ultimate goal. I will be the best player, and it won't be that long either. Now you've got one of the best players on the east coast, which is Freddie. Chicago Taylor is probably second best here in the nation's capital. Course I'm probably fourth or fifth in the DC area, probably fourth. Freddie, Chicago Taylor, and then probably Mr. Fletcher. I'm probably next. I take that back. Mr. Smoke is probably fourth. I'm probably fifth. Mr. Smoke is really, really good player. Smoke's probably the fourth player here in Washington DC metropolitan area. And I'm right after him. I don't know nobody else can beat me.

I don't have a checkers name. They just call me "Brothers." I haven't established a checkers name yet. Guys have been here a long time. They Top Masters. They got checkers names. I haven't got one as yet. Hopefully next year I will have one.

CHARLES SMOKE

DURHAM, NORTH CAROLINA (1958)

"My nickname and my last name."

Smoke

CHARLES SMOKE, 52
CAR SALESMAN, CAB DRIVER, BARBER

A lot of people play checkers forever and ever and never get to be good. Thinking ability. Thinking ability makes a good checker player. Some people have unlimited thinking ability and that's what I have, unlimited thinking ability. Some have limited thinking ability. That's the difference between a good checker player and a mediocre checker player and a non-checker player. Thinking ability. You have to start with common sense. You don't have common sense, it's going to be difficult. There's always somebody else don't have common sense too. So you play on your level, whatever that might be. You stay on that level unless you want to increase. Some people you cannot even mess with. They're not in your league.

There's a lot of people that don't mess with me. But there are a lot of people that will. So a lot of people who never played me know they can't beat me, play me anyway. Some people are in denial. Can't beat me. Won't admit it. Either way. There are all sorts of methods to the madness.

For the last six and a half years I've been selling cars. I'm a car salesman. That wears you out. Just on break right now, for a few months. I been out since March. I'll probably go back next month. I took a two-week job at another dealership and that didn't work out as planned. Sold five cars in two weeks. I worked at one, Rosenthal Nissan, for three and a half years. Rosenthal Honda for two years. So altogether almost six years in the car business.

Yellow Cab. All DC taxis work by themselves. So I'm self-employed in that sense. Yellow Cab. I have to make things work before jumping in the car business again. I tried it one more time after stopping for almost six years. A dealership. Fortunately it worked out, but it takes a lot of money by not working. Sort of like real estate, which I already liked too. You have to be ready when you get in that. Can't just jump in.

As of July 2009 I am a barber, at Mason's Hair Gallery at 1010 10th and H Streets Northeast. I went there to teach checkers and ended up being a barber. The guys from the club come around.

Fellowship is the main reason to belong to the club. You can play checkers anywhere. It's fellowship. This is like a family. And people join all the time. And people are deceased all the time. Great players. I guess it's been 15 years ago. Maybe more. Fifteen years or more. I had a guy that taught me how to play checkers. Ray Harmon, The Weasel. He taught me the game. Gave me books. He gave me lessons. He still comes to the club. This guy is highly skilled as a teacher to those who comprehend. He taught me and another young man, two or three of us. Here I am. I might be headed for the top. I don't know.

RAY HARMON

LIBERTY, NORTH CAROLINA (1949)

"The weasel's pretty slick. Steals the farmer's chickens and by the time he get out there with his gun, he's down by the river somewhere, licking his chops. I'm known to be pretty slick in checkers. Generally, I weasel out of things."

The Weasel

RAY HARMON, 61
MUSICIAN, DEPARTMENT OF EDUCATION PROGRAM ASSISTANT

In the early '70s, I stumbled on to this group of players. At that time I thought checkers was just playing and the lucky person won. I had no idea that all the strategy was involved. Everyone used to beat me in those years. I couldn't beat a soul. The guys had me playing for my little money, you know, and they would beat me out of it. There was a gentleman in the club, at the barber shop, named Booker. I used to buy his dinner every day. Our club president here, Tal Roberts, I used to pay for his haircuts. I did this until I got my hands on those books and all. Then they started to buy their own dinner and pay for their own haircuts. Now I'm one of the top players in the club.

You can't be afraid of losing. I once read it was said about Babe Ruth, "a strikeout man makes a ball player." He struck out a lot although he made a lot of home runs. So I'm thinking he was not afraid of being struck out. With checkers you can't be afraid of losing, because when you lose, you can go back and replay this game and find out why you lost it. I do that a lot. If he beats me, when I come back to play him the next time, he knows not to play that same variation.

The one guy that I have my trouble with now is the one sitting next to my left shoulder. Freddie, yeah, everybody has trouble with him. I don't know who told you, but he is probably the best in the United States. I managed to beat him once. I haven't been able to do it since.

I came to Washington just before the riots. While I was still in high school, I was coming back and forth to Washington. After completing high school I came to stay. I didn't like the jobs that I was working in Delaware. One summer, I remember working in a potato field, a corn field. I worked in chicken factories, clam factories. It was hard labor. When I come to Washington, I found that musicians could earn for a week anywhere from seventy five dollars to one hundred dollars. Back in those days it was hard for us to earn that much in a week.

I came with a rock band. We come here to do an audition at a club down around 14th and H. I think it was The Hayloft and then the group got the job at The Colt Lounge. I played guitar. The name of the band was called The Rocking Nomads. I had good success in the club life playing music for star entertainers. I played for a guy named Walter Jackson. He sang "Feeling," "Speak Her Name," and "Uphill Climb to the Bottom." He was on crutches; he had polio. He was out of Chicago. I played for a lady named Baby Washington and I played for another guy named Freddie Scott.

Next thing, someone was directing me to the Federal Government. I went to work for the Department of Education, adult education, and then I went to the Bureau of Education for the Handicapped, which eventually became Special Education. I was a program assistant. I didn't move around like a lot of people did. I just stuck it out in those two. It was exciting getting to meet all of those presidents. I shook Jimmy Carter's hand. I used to receive invitations to Inaugurals and received invitations to the White House. I saw Jimmy Carter, Reagan, Bush, the old man Bush, the Clintons. I did over 30 years. I'm retired now.

I couldn't afford to go to college and I wasn't free to be without a job. So I chose to study part time. In '92, I received my Bachelors in Business Management. In '98, I received my Masters, both at UDC (University of the District of Columbia). I tell friends I received them too late. They say, "But you got them." All I do now with all of the studying is look at them on the wall, and do income taxes.

At the club, we have a box. If you beat me five straight then I have to put a quarter in this box and you get up and go ring the bell and everybody know that you put me in the box. On the other hand, if you win four games and I win a game before you win that fifth game, then you go in the box and I get to ring the bell by just winning one game. You don't hear it that often. You only hear it say like if a strong player like myself is playing a lower rank player. Then he has the luck of ringing that bell and putting me in the box. And gets everyone to laugh at me.

DONALD CUNNINGHAM

WASHINGTON DC (1946)

"I been in there, many times, in The Box. We just laugh and have fun and put a quarter in the box. Just play again. I put people in the box too, but I been in the box many times."

The Pressure Man

Donald Cunningham, 64
Community Service Supervisor

I came in and we played checkers and I got beat pretty bad. I knew I was playing some experts when I got in this club. So I just took the beatings. Then later on my game got better because I was playing harder players. A guy that practices seven days a week, studies books on checkers, works on the computer, plays other peoples and plays tougher people. That makes your game better.

I play position. Good defense. Good offense and watch the board. That's all a person can do. Play defense and offense and watch the board. If you doing that, you might come out pretty good. Depends on who you're playing. If you're playing a top player, you can watch the board all you want and that guy will tear you up. But if you're playing somebody on your level your chances are better.

You win some, you lose some. Nobody get no attitude about they lose. Some people you can beat. Some people you can't beat. But you just keep practicing hard at it. And sooner or later you'll beat them. Just a matter of time. Main thing is who wants it the most. The game.

My mother, she used to play checkers, and I used to sit down and watch and then we started playing. Well my Mama beat me when I first started. Later on I beat her. Then I let her beat me a little more. You start off Blue Ribbon, Gold Bar, Junior Master, Master, Top Master. Just like grade school, first grade to second grade to third grade to fourth grade to fifth grade – things of that nature. I'm a Gold Bar. I didn't start on the tournaments 'til four years ago. If my mother was here, she really would enjoy that. She's deceased now. Both of them deceased, so she didn't get a chance.

I used to supervise people for years. I used to travel with Marion Barry, the mayor, back in 1967, '68 to '69, before he was mayor. An organization called Pride Incorporated on U Street. That's where I got started at, in a camp for youth. From assistant supervisor to supervisor. From a supervisor to a coordinator. From a coordinator to a community service officer. When I became a community service officer, I had my own office, my own intercom, in complete charge of the whole guys coming in the ranks. I was controller. I was on top. I supervised some of the hardest guys. Something I enjoyed doing.

When I left Pride and went to the DC government, I used to supervise ex-offenders, from Lorton prison. These guys come to see me and I put them to work, fixing guardrails that have been hit by a car. I worked in the government for 25 years. I'm retired. From there I went to the old YMCA, Prince Georges County. There I used to have different job titles. I used to drive and pick up school kids. It was a day care. Parents dropped their kids off and we take them to school and bring them back and parents come back in the evening and pick their kids up. I was in charge of the maintenance crew. I also supervised the community service people. Community service people go in courts and then have community service. They send them to me. I give them some work to do. Keep their time and hours and all that. I did that for six years.

It happened when we was comin' up, if I go out to the corner, and this lady knew my mother, she would spank me, then call my mother and say, "I gave him a beatin' 'cuz he was actin' out on the street." Those was the good days. So it is a lot different from back in the days to now. Too much goin' on now. All that killin' and all that robbin' and kids beatin' up their parents, killin' their parents, talkin' back to their parents. Stayin' out all night. Back in the '60s things were different.

JOHNNIE COLEMAN

BIRMINGHAM, ALABAMA (1945)

"I've been playing since I was four years old. I wasn't even in grade school, but I was playing grown men. Back then I played for quarters and I had my pockets full of quarters."

Johnnie Cool & Snatch

JOHNNIE COLEMAN, 65
ATHLETE, YOUTH MENTOR

I was born in Birmingham, Alabama in 1945 and came to Washington DC to go to Federal City College in 1959. It was the best place I could get my education, a BS in health education. I was an athlete: All-American football player and candidate for All-American baseball player. The origin of the name Johnnie Cool came from football and baseball. Snatch because I used to steal a lot of bases.

My number one objective in order to play checkers is not trying to scrutinize my opponent. The next step after that is you try to have profound understanding of checkers, to use strategies, positions. You got to position yourself on the board. If you uptight and try to win immediately, you're defeating your own purpose. Go for your draw first.

For a win on a small board, you get two points. For a loss, you get zero points. For a draw, you get one point. So a draw is important. When you sit down at the board don't try to beat nobody. Try to get draws and then position yourself. If you see you can possibly win something, go in and win it. I guarantee you will be a checker champ.

I was a Master before my time because I have held championships in Indiana, came in second place repeatedly. I had held championships in the District of Columbia, Virginia, Maryland, North Carolina, Alabama. We got a couple checker players in this club very, very competitive and can play anywhere in the world against anybody. Against anybody. Now that's the ultimate in checkers, "Hey how far can you go?"

Some of the tournaments you play in the United States, guess what? They pay you. I think the maximum purse you can get in a tournament is two or three thousand dollars. But the purse gets larger and larger for playing in the major tournaments. It's so amazing! All the tournaments are played in the Holiday Inn. So you see how big it is, right? We play in the Holiday Inn. On the other hand, back in years ago, we used to play in the shade tree. Not in, no, it was unheard of playing in a Holiday Inn. Back then, under a shade tree, soda tops and a homemade board. Now we play on custom-made boards. The Lord's been good to us.

Mr. Hill, a much older guy, he died a year or so ago. He used to go all over the United States, he was age 90, to record them games, to pass them back to others, for to help them build their games up. He was a Master checker player as well as Dog Green [William Green], a cofounder. Checkers Club was found in 1986 or '84 and was over on 7th Street. Main drag. A barber shop. He was one of the most highly respected and prominent checkers player here in Washington DC. He was Top Master as well as Mr. Pat Foster. All the guys just took me under their wing and helped build my game up. And Mr. Tal Roberts, president, is only the second president we had.

I'm a community-oriented person. I run "Mentors of Future Athletes of Seat Pleasant," a football and baseball camp for kids in Seat Pleasant, Maryland that been going on since 1996. We offer summer reading in the park, Easter egg roll for kids, and taking kids to tournaments all around the United States during the summer. We pick up food from the churches and the community centers and pass it right on to the kids. Mostly one parent families. So we're very committed to doing things for the neighborhood.

Sad to say. Sad to say. Our enrollment has declined big time. Now some of them, some of our more prominent players, have died out, like World War II Veterans, while the younger generation want football, basketball. They want smoke that reefer, right?

MIKE WEAVER

"When I first came to the club, another player was beating me pretty easily and after a short time here, I learned how to play and I beat him. So he nicknamed me 'Boy Wonder.'"

Boy Wonder

MIKE WEAVER, 39
COMMERCIAL TRUCK DRIVER

I've been interested in checkers forever. Since I was young, playing in elementary school, H.D. Cooke Elementary, at recess. I immediately took a liking to the game and I found that I was good at it. DC was more modern than where I lived in Jamaica, and it was winter when I arrived. I remember it being pretty cold. Yes. I was nasty cold. As a small boy, I had to walk to school. I remember those cold days.

Once I found out they played on the streets, I started going to the areas where they played. They used to play down at the Giant on 9th Street. Checkers is played everywhere, like guys playing basketball. You just have to find some little spot to play at. Some barber shops they play. So wherever they played at, I try to find those places, and then go there. Then I ran into a couple of players who played exceptionally well and I played them. I wanted to find out how they learned how to play checkers as good as they do. So that's when I found out about the Checkers Club. Charles Smoke. He told me about this club. He was playing at a cab stand. I met him at a cab stand. Just have to ask around, ask the guys who play checkers. And they'll show you. They said to come by any time and they'd teach me. So I did.

Now I'm Gold Bar. I won the Blue Ribbon the last time I played, won the tournament. That's like the National Tournament. I won the Blue Ribbon title, so now I have to move up. It's mandatory that I move up. Gold Bar. So that's where I'm at. Gold Bar.

During the '80s and '90s, DC went through a pretty rough period. Pretty hard. Kind of like the crack generation then. In school, they preached about it. Preached and preached. It stuck in my head. That and along with the fact that I saw a lot of it in my neighborhood and I saw the effects of it on the people who used it. Those experiences told me not to bother with it. It brought about the potential to make some money for the guys who sold the drugs, but the middle class started using crack, you know, pretty bad. The streets in DC, 20 years ago, some of the roughest dudes in the city wouldn't dare tread in the daytime, much less at night. Now even two in the morning, open their doors at night in those areas. So I guess you could say some of it is an improvement.

I drive a dump truck. Class B commercial, all trucks except tractor-trailers. I like it 'cuz you're out all during the day. So the day goes by pretty quickly. A sense of accomplishment that you complete all that work. So that's what I like about it. Good pay. It's not great, but I want to start my own trash company.

DC have their own style and that's what I like about it. The slang, the lingo and things like that. The mannerisms of the people here is different here than other places. What was startling to me was how, in other cities, how friendly they were. I wasn't used to that, living in DC. Here they kinda like more watching out for, you know, whatever moves, somebody might try to break. That kind of thing keeps you on your toes. Keeps you pretty sharp, not as gullible, you know. That's what I like about DC.

The first time I came to the club, I ran into one of the toughest players they have, Chicago Taylor. And he beat me five games. And then he gave me pointers about what I was doing wrong with the game and talked a lot of junk to me and made me want to learn to play. So, that was the first time. Chicago Taylor got a hold of me. You have to analyze. And you also have to control urges to move quickly without thinking. So you have to be patient. I had to train myself to resist the impulses to move without thinking about all the possibilities. I had to learn that.

Thomas Franklin Webber

WASHINGTON DC (1954)

"I have a distinguished way. I'll get them in a game and I say, in a higher voice, "Come here John." When they hear that noise, they know the little boy is in trouble. He's hungry."

Come Here John

Thomas Franklin Webber, 56

MUSICIAN, BUSINESS OWNER

Saturdays when I'm not traveling with the groups, if I'm in town, I'm predicting I can be found here. The Missus – she doesn't mind at all. She says, "He's not womanizing; I know where he's at. He's right here." So it's good. It's a wholesome game we play. We talk some talk sometime, like men, you know, but I love this bunch. If it weren't for them, I don't know where I would be.

I play keyboard since I was 13. I do R&B. I worked with jazz artist called Jimmy Summers. I worked out on the road for about six years with Wilson Picket, as his keyboarder. That money was good. Paid all the bills. But it just keeps you away from home. And trying to do a young marriage, which I tried, too much time away from the post, brings dissention. I worked with the Coasters - was singing "Yaketey Yak" and "Charlie Brown." Recently worked with Jean Carne, who's a jazz vocalist also. I do the tours with her and do it with a writer called Michael Henderson and Norman Conners who writes for a lot of people. So I work with them also. It's a good feeling when you're riding in the car and you listen to 105.9 and here's a man you play for and here his music comes on and I hear it and it makes me feel good. Because at the point in my life a lot of things were happening when I got exposed to this club. Kind of coming out of a troubled marriage. I could have taken some roads that was available but they wouldn't have been no good for me. And there were folks around who was doing … influence of drugs. And I said, "I don't want to do this. What do I do? I got to find something I can enjoy that is just plain and simple and not expensive." And I came across an old friend of the family and he said, "Come on in here young boy, and let's see what you know." I had such a good time getting beat, I said, "I'll be back." And I came back.

One of the things I really am concerned with, this game become extinct to young folks. All the fun we have here, all this knowledge of the game. I went to Jamaica, Trinidad. They still play this.

This is one of the cheapest games. A lot of people take this to not to be that strong of a game compared to chess. They put chess way above. I play both. I play both on a high level. One is not too much more strategic than the other.

Our game doesn't get the exposure. I guess chess is played mostly over in Europe, in Britain, France and so forth and it came under royalty pastime, so it's got a higher status than us. This came out of slavery thing and so forth; they could afford this. It is an easier piece to make than it is for somebody who wants to play chess. So easy.

My father played checkers. When he retired from his job with the federal government, he wanted something to do so he took over a barber shop that was failed and a checkerboard was in there. He was kind of like a hero type person to me. The barber shop was on 9th and West Virginia Avenue, Northeast Washington. It was Webbers Barber Shop at the time. He retired along '74 and kept that barber shop 'til about '84. He was a country boy and they liked to play checkers. They like to talk stuff. During that time there were certain guys around. They had a street lottery. They did their business there, and so the barber shop was a meeting place. In any town you see in the old days, the barber shop was the hang out.

I'm kinda like the club comedian. We had a little joke. I do R&B. I tease Mr. Taylor about it all the time. And I told Mr. Taylor, I said, "You could grow up the gospel business to all great heights if Highway QC's and Little Richard teamed up together." And he looked at me and he shook his head, "NO, I might lose my customers." But I said, I would tease him. I would say, "Chi, if your group all came out and the piano player be there *da da da da da*. 'Ladies and Gentleman. Highway QC's and featuring *whooo-whoooo-whooo* Little Richard.'" He canned my idea. But the guys thought it was a good idea. "We going to stay strictly religious," he said. "Little Richard might slip." So it's just our little thing. I tease him with it.

SPENCER TAYLOR

INDIANOLA, MISSISSIPPI (1928)

"I remember I was reluctant to beat my father, but he told me "No." He wanted to see me advance and he knew when I got so I could beat him. Though he didn't know nothing about the game, he was the best for a long time. I give him a lot of credit."

Chicago

Spencer Taylor, 82

I started at an early age trying to learn, my father and I, in Mississippi. My Dad got me interested in checkers. At that time, he could beat everybody in the house, naturally, and then I kept on until I could beat everybody. It was just something just caught me. It was quite competitive and quite interesting. As time went on, I continued to get better and better and better. I had an older brother, my older brother, could play. At one time he was better naturally, 'cuz he was older. But as time went on I caught up with everybody so I ended up the better player out of the family.

Singing is my profession. That's what I do. Still do. Highway QC's, gospel singing. We started out, back in Chicago, as teenagers, as a group. And this highway came from a church that some of us belong to at that time and the QC's came from a little school, the initials at that time. QC's. So we put it together, trying to be different and came up with the name Highway QC's. We started out with five people. I'm the only original now. Everything was a cappella. We go everywhere. I go all over the country singing. I started living here in '64 and been here ever since. Earlier in life, I was a clerk in the main Post Office in Chicago. Opportunity presented itself and I took it and I haven't been back.

We was like running from North Carolina, South Carolina, Virginia and up to New York City on up, Connecticut and back down like as far as Georgia and all the southern states. But each time, I think it look like we needed a replacement and we was up this way so much. Then one day I decided, all my work was up here and I moved up here. I changed on account of all the work – the Apollo Theater. We also did Madison Square Garden, Carnegie Hall. All those things. Actually my singing put me up here. My singing actually put me in DC. It was more convenient. It fit in. That's how I got here.

I like DC. All my family, my wife, kids, grandkids and friends are here. I've created a lot of friends. A friend of mine back in Chicago said to me one day, we were there, and he asked me why don't I move back to Chicago? And I said, "Well I wouldn't know anyone but you. You be the only person I know here." He laughed 'cuz he realized that I been gone that long. Basically I wouldn't know anybody. That's a long time and you accumulate so many friends, so many friends, so many. So I like it. I love it DC, to live here. I don't know any place else to go. I'd stay here. I don't like Florida. I don't like Arizona. I been to all those places. I like to go, sing, and leave. I like to go to Vegas, sing and leave. I like to go to California, sing and leave.

Anything in life you do, and you're really good, I'm really grateful. I'm very grateful that I learned the game quite well. You win more than you lose. Then you make a name for yourself. You do well and you make a name. It's a lot of fun. There's fun in it. You come in and everybody "Hey Chicago" or whatever. Mostly a lot of people know about straight checkers. The only checker on the board that can move backward is the king in straight checkers. In this Spanish pool checkers you jump to your advantage with this game. There are jumps that come up that you must take. Everything else is different. We have restrictions too, but jump to your advantage. You jump to your advantage.

A good checker player learns the game. The entire game. The rules. That's going to be first. If you learn that, then you're on your way. Calm. Good mind. Solid thinking. Good thinking ability. People with strong brains can analyze. Some people analyze better than others. We have to face that. Some people seem that they are slower, but that's not true. They analyze very deep. They look at everything. I might look at it too quick. Like life. A lot of things going on in life. You could take time. I might be too fast. That's my theory.

PERNELL LEE

SOUTH NORFOLK, VIRGINIA (1936)

"I don't take any prisoners. I go straight for the jugular vein. I have no mercy on those persons that I'm playing."

Butt Kicker

69

Pernell Lee, 74
Barber, Business Owner

My father was an excellent checker player. I used to watch him and that's how I learned. I didn't beat my Dad, not while he was in his prime. My Dad died at 98. When he got over 95, I could beat him every now and then.

He was from Norfolk, Virginia. He was the best of Norfolk. They had no checkers club in Norfolk that I know of, but people used to have checkers games in barber shops and in their homes. He used to go there to play and they used to come to our house and play, sometimes half the night. At that time they didn't have any nicknames as we do. They said he was "the best." And that's how they referred to him, as being The Best.

Washington DC was bigger than Norfolk. More things to do and more things that needed to be done. Right off I saw the business possibilities in Washington. I came to DC to go to Howard University, to study chemistry. My first place I lived was in the dormitory at Howard University, called Lucy Diggs Slowe Hall. 1955 – 1959. It cost $30.00 a month, and meals cost 40 cents a meal. It's on 3rd Street Northwest. My wife and I married in the chapel at Howard University.

When I was in high school I started cutting hair to supplement my expenses. While I was at Howard, I was a barber. There was a barber shop in Cook Hall at Howard that I tried to buy, but wasn't successful there. Later I bought a barber shop, Lee's Barber Shop, 5313 Georgia Avenue Northwest. We played in the barber shop. Our customers would come in and see us playing and then they would start playing. And then they would come in the barber shop for the exclusive purpose of playing checkers. I owned the shop for about ten years and we played checkers the whole ten years that I was there.

My barber shop had five chairs and five barbers. Pops, Robert Jones, Mr. Moore and Mr. Hargrove were the barbers. We cut men and women's hair. For the women we also did their eyebrows and gave facial massages with a mudpack. For the men we trimmed mustaches and cut their hair. I also started the Barbers and Beauticians Club. We bought supplies directly from the wholesaler and bypassed the middleman. Our store was the District Barber and Beauty

Supply in the store on Georgia Avenue next to Cunningham's Barber Shop. Mr. Cunningham owned the building. East side of street, 5400 block, two story tan building. We sold stock to the barbers and beauticians in the area. The business was good until the riots of 1968. When Martin Luther King was assassinated, the District was destroyed. It was 20-25 years before it started coming back.

From there I started my own business of carpet cleaning, window cleaning. Then I was a private contractor for many years, and vacuum cleaner repair business also. And that was how I spent my working life. Now I'm somewhat retired. I still go out every day doing things, but not as much as I used to. I don't have the pressure that I used to have. At one time we had three kids in college, a house note, two cars. But now there's nobody in college, no house note. So I'm somewhat relaxed now. I go to bed when I want to. Get up when I want to.

I find that there are people who have PhDs can't play checkers. You would think these people would be able to play better than those who drive cabs or park cars for a living but this is not the case. Some of the best players I've seen haven't finished high school. And I cannot figure out how they are able to play better than those who have had years and years of experience in education. I don't know myself. Maybe they have certain gifts in this direction. That's the way it goes.

PATRICK FOSTER

KANSAS CITY, MISSOURI (1930s)

*"My on-line name when I wanted to be mysterious.
But the fellows found me out."*

Danny O'Shea of Ireland

PATRICK FOSTER, 70s
PHYSICIST

My interest in checkers basically started when I was in school, going to graduate school up at Howard. And I was stopped at a service station, and these elderly fellows were there playing, and they just beat me up. And I couldn't understand it. I said, "Here I am, you know, in school, working on my doctorate, and I couldn't understand how they could beat me so easily."

The high school I went to was very small. A small southern school. My graduating class was like about 30. And when I reached the 12th grade, they offered, for the first time, a course called physics. For the first time. They wanted me to go into medicine. I saw how hard those people had to work. Those doctors had to make house calls. Not that I'm against hard work. I just said, "Doesn't appeal to me." Just something like this, you know, in life how things come to you. Some things are hard, some things are easy. Physics came with ease.

I went to Howard University, a PhD in Physics in the '60s. My work was in physics-underwater acoustics. I worked at the David Taylor Model Basin. It was with naval ships. Detection, trying to be quieter than the next guy, so you can hear him first. Means you can shoot first. We used models of ships and submarines to test, but there's a towing basin called a model basin that rises off the tracks that can pull models of ships through the water. It is interesting. The railing of that facility follows the curvature of the earth. Seems like at least three quarters of a mile long. I know we used to go in there and walk, for exercise. That was not a good idea because they had asbestos packing for soundproofing.

Playing checkers is some kind of spatial, two-dimensional visualization and having objectives. Essentially it is a battlefield. You look at it that way. Knowing ahead of time, developing tactics to achieve those objectives and just those simple kind of battlefield concepts.

At some point I started subscribing to magazines from Russia, Soviet Russia. Mostly a lot of the literature was in Russian, which is a very different script, and I had no chance in understanding that. But they published a magazine. We use a common notation for recording checker games, so that language I could pretty much follow. It's the alphanumeric system, which is A1, B2, etc. At the time I was working for the Defense Department and I am sure that my mail was being scrutinized because it was coming from Russia. I subscribed to their magazine for about 20 years. There was very little literature on our form of checkers written by American authors during that time.

They really push tournaments here. They try to have as big a group as possible, so they can have those bragging rights, "We have the most from Washington." Washington includes Baltimore. Turns out the prize money that you win won't even cover your costs. But you know, even that, they look at it as being important. I kinda got away from competitive checkers about 20 years ago. Now it's just a fellowship thing that I come down to join the guys, and *whoop* and *holler*.

JOHN A. WILLIAMS III

BALTIMORE, MARYLAND (1941)

"Sometimes I be sittin' in the Square all day, you know, my stomach's all a growlin', playin' checkers. That's how much I loved it."

Buck

John A. Williams III, 69
BUSINESS OWNER, GENERAL CONTRACTOR

Freddie Owens. Most of the time he beat me. 90% of the time he beat me. I enjoy playing with him. I really enjoy playing with him. He makes the game interesting, plus it help me. I like to play a lot of different types of games and he help me out. Makes me stronger too. So he help me to win a game or two.

I was about 15 years old when I started playing. That's how I met Freddie. Playing checkers. We used to play at Franklin Square in Baltimore and then winter time come and we started playing in each other's house and we got better and better. If we lost a game, we would set it up and analyze. That helped us play better and by both of us doing the same thing, our game got strong over the winter months. When the summer come, we went up to the Square. We had improved and started beatin' on 'em. Me and Freddie.

I started at Franklin Square and wound up playing up in Harlem Square. That's where the better players were. When they got a checker club, we started studying the books, and then we started beatin' some of the guys that was older than us. They got so they didn't want to play us. After all that studying over the years, night and day. I had studied 10 and 12 hours a day, like I'm going to work.

My mother said I don't see what you see in playing them checkers. But it was something I liked. I used to be in the house, playing. You hear something - pit pit pit pit pit pit pat - and my mother go, "Oh Lordy, there he go again." Eventually I quit school; I came out when I got 16. I learned a trade like paintin' and wall paperin', plasterin', put up sheet rock and all that. I worked for myself, when I was 19 years old. And when I wasn't working, I be playing checkers. I used to sneak out of the house. Sneak out the house in the morning and sneak in when I come back in at night. I didn't want to do nothing but play checkers. I didn't even want to work. My mama used to get on me sometimes because when I work, I use to help out. So eventually I got my head together and when jobs came in, I had to go do them and just play checkers when I was able to play. In the evening, or on Saturday, when I wasn't working.

I had a good memory. I used to study when them tests come up – English, math, social studies, geography. Sometimes I make 85 on a test. But my favorite game was checkers. So that's what I done, play checkers. Every chance I got. I would be walking the street with nothing but checkers on my mind. I lost a girlfriend behind checkers. They have a little tournament in the shoeshine place, right where they shine shoes, and they have a little tournament, and when I came home, it was all over. The girl quit me, found somebody else. I was hurt, you know. Yep.

I used to play Mr. George Briscoe at that time. He was the best checker player in Baltimore at that time. After I started getting good, I started playin' for money. Twenty-five dollars a game. Sometimes he beat me one week and I beat him the next week. That's how it goes, seesaw. He didn't want to play nobody unless they played for money. Ain't no limit to how much they would play for. Eventually I start playin' for tournaments. So far I won like about eight trophy. I won the Gold Bar. I won Junior Master. And I won the Master.

Curtis found me when I just get ready to come back to checkers. That's when I ran into Curtis. I realize I was getting older and that's why I came back to checkers, in ' 99. When I came back, Curtis introduced me to the computer. It helped my game a lot, studyin' the computer. You cannot beat the computer. The computer has helped my game. I get straighten out with my false teeth, when I get my teeth in, then I start working on savin' some money for a brand new computer this time. I got a disc already. So I can't wait 'til I get a computer.

WILLIAM DeSHIELDS

CAMDEN, DELAWARE (1927)

"I'm the worst checkers player."

Wolf Street

81

WILLIAM DeSHIELDS, 83
LONGSHOREMAN, CRANE OPERATOR

I really had no interest in checkers, but I started going with the club in '99, with the checkers players. I had a house, 2310 East Preston Street, in Baltimore. The fellas played in garages and alleys and the squares and it started to get cold and I told them they could come to the house 'cuz there wasn't anybody there but I. And so then we started a checkers club in '99.

I had a great big sign and these type of lights in the window, and you could see it two blocks away. EAST BALTIMORE CHECKERS CLUB. The fellas used to come down there and they was friendly, just like here. Come here and play checkers. Don't matter you win or lose. We always had sodas. Sometimes I just get my daughter, and other ladies that I knew, just to cook up a great big pot of soup, or cook up some chicken, or something like that, and I mean it was like one family, one big family. Like it is here. After we started the club, we got in touch with some of the fellows over in DC, this club right here, the Capital Club.

DeShields is an old name, a French name. I spell it with capital "D." My grandmother was 119 when she passed. I am from Camden, Delaware, but there was very little work to be done in Camden. I was drafted on March 14, '46. I was in the Air Force. A machinist, cutting steel into various parts and shapes. Very exciting. Very dangerous too. Have to keep your mind on what you are doing. We made different types of gears for the F85 and F86 fighter planes. They had trouble with landing gears releasing when hitting the ground. We had to lock them in place; make them stiffer when they hit. I was stationed overseas – Korea, Yokohama, Japan, Tokyo and last place was Clark Field, Luzon, Philippines. I wasn't on the aircraft carrier. I worked on the beach in the machine shop. I didn't know about machinery before.

I was in for three years and two days – can't leave out my days. Can't pin down to hours and minutes and seconds. I was ready to get out. I never was used to somebody telling you everything you do. You might be laying in the bunk reading a book and the sergeant of the barracks come and click the lights out. Doesn't matter. You have to scramble around and get your nightclothes and so forth. Get in your bunk. So I never liked that. So that's the reason I was always glad when my time comes to get out.

I come to Baltimore after I come out of the Service, after World War II, in 1949. I got a job as a longshoreman and I started working for Bethlehem Steel – Sparrows Point. Crane operator. Locomotive crane operator. The crane that runs up and down the tracks like the railroad engines. I did that, then I transferred to the open hearth where they make steel, on the BOF floor. I got burned a couple of times but I got over that. I worked down there 32 years and then retired on disability. Pretty good union, the CIO.

In '85, '86 I took sick. I was in the hospital and after I came out of the hospital they sent me back to work and on my job. They didn't have no light duty, but I come back on duty on the same job. But what happened was when they sent me back to work, I couldn't pick up five pounds for 10 million dollars. I was just that weak. But that was when the clause in the union book, was that I had to go back to work for nine months, to see if I could actually do my job. I went back to work for nine months, but I couldn't do it. I've been on disability since March the 28th, 1987. I was 60 years old then.

The house in Baltimore got burned down in '05. We don't have a club now. That's why I've been sticking with this club here. I've been traveling with them every time they have a tournament. I didn't play, just went with the crowd.

Fletcher Clark

BALTIMORE, MARYLAND (1929)

"I beat a lot of people."

The Champ

FLETCHER CLARK, 81
IRON WORKER

Take a special kind of person, you know, running these kind of clubs, you know, keep it going, you know, like Tal Roberts. He got a little education. He got a little what cha call it? Like people at the head of the things, they sort of devoted you know. Everybody can't run it. No. You got followers and you got people who like to be in the lead, a head of things.

I put 30 years on at Sparrows Point in Baltimore. We made iron really, then they turned iron into steel. But our outfit was more or less like the first operation. Then it left our department and went to another department and they changed the stage of it. Hot work. Hot. Dirty.

I wore long drawers year round and you'd be surprised but the clothes keep the heat off. Like if I was around something real hot and I just had pants on, these pants would burn my legs. Get hot. Even if you stand by the side of the stove. If you got thin things on, they get hot and burn you. But now if you had an undershirt underneath of that, your clothes wouldn't burn you. And see, we had clothes just like the fire department. The clothes the fire department got on, they don't catch afire. They get hot.

The tournaments. You say good luck to me? I need it. I need it to be victorious. We play people all over the world and you find yourself burning the midnight oil you know. I wake up sometimes at two o'clock in the night and get my checkerboard and play to about four or five in the morning. You know they doing the same thing. It ain't easy. Not easy.

You know some people, you know, you haven't seen them all year, you know, and they come. It's a week of checkers and you get a belly full of checkers. You get a belly full.

I play mostly every chance I get. But I practice too, you know, on the board I have at home. With symbols. Try to remember, that's the main thing. Got to have a good mind. Good memory. Good mind. Everybody don't have that. I played checkers since a kid, but then I got serious when I got to be a man.

A lot of people play checkers. But there's different grades of checkers. People think they can play checkers, but they never study, so you're not going to beat, not studying books, and you just playing. Can't accomplish too much. You got to learn from other people. Some people play on the street but they don't play by the rules. You come here, they play by the rules and then they got a purpose. It's a higher grade of checkers. They try to get better and better. It's probably just like playing cards. When them guys play on television. That's a different grade of card player than the average person. We all know how to play cards. But playing cards with them? Not have a chance.

TONY SIMUEL

COLUMBIA, SOUTH CAROLINA (1950s)

"When I am playing checkers it is like pounding nails."

The Hammer

TONY SIMUEL, 50s
ARMY INTELLIGENCE, BUSINESS OWNER

I learned checkers by watching the older men in my father's barber shop play, in Columbia, South Carolina. Up here I used to go to Dupont Circle and play chess. While I was down there, one gentleman come with a checkerboard and set it up and I beat him. So he said, "You need to go down to the club and play."

The first time I came, I met Tal. He was walking a man through the club and he say, "Hey, we got a lot of good players here." The gentleman over there, Freddie, he's an outstanding player. In fact he's the best in this region. I know he's the best from New York down to here. And I don't think there's much playing up farther than that. But all the way down to North Carolina and Georgia. I'm hoping to beat Freddie.

You don't know that yet. Freddie, I'm talking about you.

It takes patience and concentration and studying. I have a lot of patience, I have a lot of concentration, but I don't have time to study. And now that I have the books, I don't have the time.

My strength is position. I'm not going to tell you my weakness because these guys, when they find your weakness, they work on you. As I said about Freddie, they write down his games. Clarence Gooche, he got a database in his computer and he's also getting a lot of information about the Russians and he's sharing it with us. He came from North Carolina just to do that and that's good.

That guy there, Spencer Taylor, he's a super star gospel singer, big time.

Spencer, How you doing there? All right? Just talking about you.

I come once a week. Well, I try and come once a week. I was in intelligence in the Army, for 20 years, at Bolling Air Force Base. Now I am self-employed in commercial cleaning. But if I could, I be down here everyday. I like to come daily, but being married and the wife, and she already called here saying, "Don't stay there too long now." I think you know how that is.

I want to stay here, but I have my wife who has other plans. She wants go back to South Carolina or Georgia, back to her family, most of her family. We're here right now, but I don't know what's going to happen in the next couple of years.

Obama is for change. He's for change. I actually think that he really means to bring people together. That's good. That's how we solve problems that we have in the world. To have people working together.

JAMES B. DIXON

FAYETTEVILLE, NORTH CAROLINA (1927)

"I like checkers because I like competition and it's an individual sport. If you lose, it's on you. Nobody can help you. Shake hands. Play. Game's over. Shake hands."

Kid Dixon

James B. Dixon, 83
CAB DRIVER, TELECOMMUNICATIONS SPECIALIST

I'm really excited about Barack Obama. But when I was growing up, my only hero was Joe Louis. You ever hear of him? He was a champion. I was 10 years old when he won the championship. He was my hero. Before that, Jesse Owens won the Olympics. The only kind of people I looked up to.

It's amazing I even had the desire to go to school because both of my parents went to the seventh grade. When I started to read, like I saw a light. I had a thirst. I wanted to learn more. I had a thirst for knowledge. But down there we had to go to a separate but equal school. That's what they call it. Separate. Equal. I didn't learn a thing. They told me I was the smartest thing. You see the teachers would leave the room, say, "Take charge." They come through your neighborhood with a bus and you had to go six miles down the road to a school. Separate but equal and the teachers didn't know anything to teach. I guess it wasn't their fault.

I thought I was great, until I got to Howard. They say, "You have to go back to remedial." Reading remedial. I was an A student down there and then they put me back in everything. I had to start from scratch. I had to burn the midnight oil to have a 2.5, or they put me out of school. That was rough. So I mean I could've gone from elementary school to college, and learned nothing. Not a thing. That's sad, isn't it? But I thought I was hot stuff. An A student. Until I got to Howard and they knocked me down. Back then, in the day, Howard University, for a Black person, was like going to Harvard. Everybody wanted to go there. Tal, the president of this club, went to Howard University at the same time as me.

Where I come from, they had a sign "You go over here," "You go over there." In the South everybody has an idea to go North – New York, Philadelphia – anywhere, but just go North. I got here. I said, "I made it." I thought I had died and gone to heaven because I saw Black people on the street laughing, talking and having fun, and nobody was telling them what to do.

Back in the '50s, I used to drive a cab, the Dixie Cab Company, at 6th and Rhode Island Avenue. At the cab station, we had a checker stand. We played in between trips.

I became very proficient. I was good. I was the best thing in the house. My wife and I owned the cab and the company, Dixie Cab. Started in '48, 1948. The last time I renewed my license was '74 because I drove the cab and went to school at the same time. In fact, for a while after we got married, my wife drove a cab too. It was rough. She was babysitting one of our sons driving the cab. She was 40 years old when she went back to school. She got her Master's degree. That's determination, isn't it? Both of us had a license, so we could take turns driving.

I was a telecommunications specialist. I took care of communications for districts all over the country. I'd have to go out to New York, Philadelphia, Cincinnati, Seattle setting up communications systems. It was exciting. It wasn't like sitting at a desk all day. That'd be boring. Travel, I enjoyed that. I worked until I was 68 years old. I retired in '95 and my wife retired the same year and we walked off into the sunset together. Isn't that romantic? It's very romantic isn't it? Last month we went out to celebrate our 58th wedding anniversary. Eight years ago we celebrated our 50th wedding anniversary. We got married again and the same pastor that married us the first time did the ceremony again. He died since then.

I went to work for the government for 40 years and then came back to checkers. I don't play very well. A couple guys here, most of the guys here are Masters. The guy you just got through talking with, he's a Master in chess and checkers, plus he's a musician. I've seen him in concert. Charles Covington. He says he semi-retired with chess, so he's trying to perfect his checker game. He's a perfectionist. I'm not.

CHARLES COVINGTON

BALTIMORE, MARYLAND (1941)

"Everything has patterns. In music, you have patterns. In chess and checkers, you have patterns. In life, you have patterns."

Master of Disaster

Charles Covington, 69

MUSICIAN, MAGICIAN, PROFESSOR

I had already been a chess Master for years and I was thinking that checkers would be easy. So one day I decided to play and everybody beat up on me. I used to go to a club in Baltimore and everybody used to beat me all the time. I used to hear them talk about Freddie all the time. So I found out where he lived and I went to his house. He wouldn't play me right away. It took weeks. Eventually we started playing and I started studying.

I heard a couple of old players were playing down at the Waxter Center in Baltimore. A year or so ago I went down there. I said, "Do you remember me?" "Oh yeah. We used to beat up on you all the time." So now the tables are turned.

With checkers, I just say I'm an expert. When I'm out competing, it's Top Masters. The reason I advance so quickly is because I study. In order to play on a top level you have to study. Most of these guys they don't study. They just play. What makes checkers so different from chess is all the pieces are simple. They all look alike. So it's very simple. The rules are simple. It's very easy to learn, but it takes a lifetime to master.

If I had started when I was younger, I would have been a prodigy. I had an unusual story. I think I was born with perfect pitch, like I could hear anything. I had a very abusive father, so I didn't really start anything until I was about 18. At 19, I went into the service. All of a sudden I could learn anything. I could pick up things just like that. I was like a sponge. I was just learning everything I could. I blossomed out.

I'm a chess player, a checkers player, musician, magician and professor. All of those are my professions, but they also are my hobbies. It's good when you do professionally things that you like. I'm also an artist, a student of mathematics, Chinese chess (*Xiangqi*), and Japanese chess (*Shogi*), but actually Chinese chess is probably harder than chess and checkers together. It's very complex. In chess and checkers you get to create. Just like in music you get to create. The main thing they all have in common is patterns.

The start of my music career was while I was in the service. Army. The military band. I would listen to them and sometimes they would let me sit in. My music skills advanced quickly, so in three years I was playing as well as all of the greats. So I started out in good company. Now I'm playing with all the greats: Dorothy Donegan, Ruth Brown, Herbie Hancock, B. B. King, Chuck Berry, Kenny Burrell, Abbey Lincoln, Sammy Davis, Jr., Eartha Kitt and many more.

I have been teaching jazz piano at Howard University, since 1992. Before that I taught at Peabody Conservatory of Music in Baltimore for 20 years, from '79 to '99. I am the first African American to teach there. Prior to that they didn't allow Blacks to teach. If you wanted to study with a professor, you had to go to his house. I was excited when I first came to Washington because all the great musicians were playing over here at Howard Theater. Count Basie, Duke Ellington, Ella Fitzgerald, Jimmy Smith.

I have books of chess, mathematics, and music. You name it; I have a book on it. At home, I've got the largest checker library in the United States. There's two kinds of education. Education that somebody gives you and education that you give yourself. It's usually the best kind.

FREDDIE OWENS

BALTIMORE, MARYLAND (1942)

"I see a lot on the board, like a hawk."
The Hawk

101

FREDDIE OWENS, 68

MACHINE OPERATOR, JANITOR

I started when I was about 16. I used to play out in the Square over in Baltimore, after I got out of school. Watching guys play. Got real interested in the game. I began to study the game. Got a hold of some books and kept studying and studying, trying to improve my game to get better all the time.

I been playing I guess like about 50 years. Back in the '60s, we was at a barber shop. I just love the game. Anywhere I would find out there was players, I would go and play them, challenge them. I enjoy the challenge of it. It was more popular back in the '60s, '70's and early '80s. We had a lot more players for one thing. Since then a lot of guys have passed away. Every time we lose a player we lose a part of the game, really. The game goes down a notch.

I came to DC just for checkers mainly, because I heard they had a lot of players in DC and I wanted to play. I used to go anywhere I heard they had players. I played in Baltimore too and make trips to New York to play. I started playing tournaments in 1972. I became Top Master in 1972.

I like to play regularly. It helps me keep in good playing condition. I feel if you lay off the game for a long while your timing is off balance. And checkers is mainly timing. If you make your moves at the right time you got a much better chance of keeping control of the game. And once your timing is off you lose your balance. Game can go any kind of way once you lose your timing.

The main strategy is to try and control the center of the board. That's the main idea of checkers. The more you can control the center of the board, the better chance you have to win. It's sort of like a war. Sort of like a war. Trying to out think the other man. And you have to play according to what the other person is playing. So really what you're doing is responding to his rules. You have to count on the other player's moves. But you have to try to do it in advance, before it gets on the board. The farther in advance as you can do it, the better you can play. If you can analyze five moves before it gets on the board that helps you a lot. That's one of the main ideas. If you can get a draw out of a complicated position, squeeze out a draw, that makes you feel good too, when you can do that.

I would say it's a very exciting, entertaining game once you really get into it. There's no limit to what actually can be learned or played. Always something new can come up on the board. I thought it was limited at one time, but now, since I started getting advanced information, I see there is no limit to it.

CITY GAME

Freddie Owens says this is a standard, advanced game pattern and it comes up a lot. *City Game* means the strongest playing is in the middle of the board. Freddie played this game in 1970 in a checkers club on North Carrollton Avenue in Baltimore, MD. Freddie had the first move and he won. Black moves first.

Regulation Setup

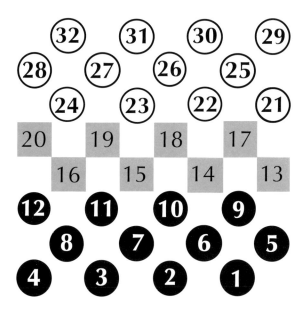

City Game

LEGEND

- *equals* Slide

x *equals* Jump

?? *equals* Move that lost the Game

NOTE: Black moves first

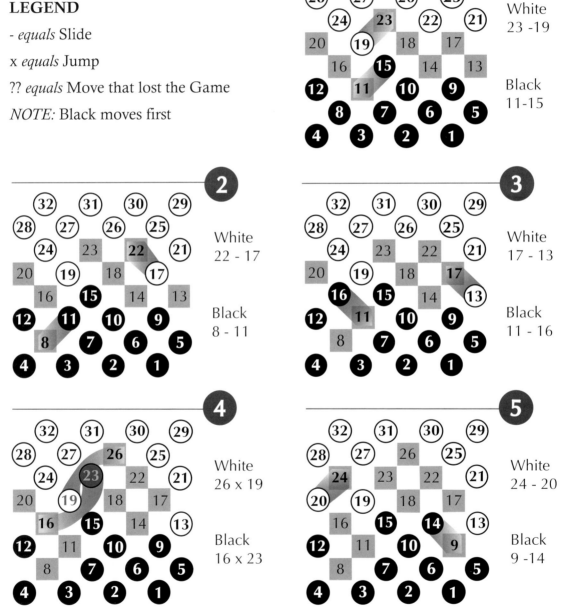

1

White
23 -19

Black
11-15

2

White
22 - 17

Black
8 - 11

3

White
17 - 13

Black
11 - 16

4

White
26 x 19

Black
16 x 23

5

White
24 - 20

Black
9 -14

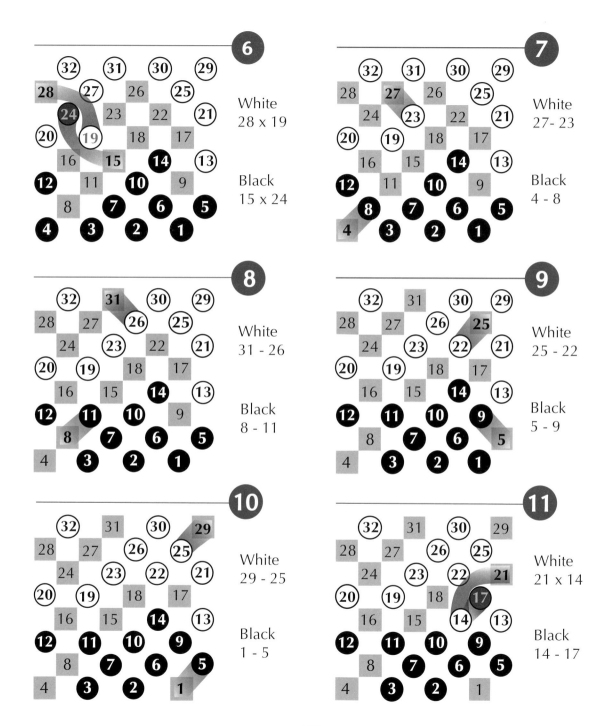

6

White
28 x 19

Black
15 x 24

7

White
27- 23

Black
4 - 8

8

White
31 - 26

Black
8 - 11

9

White
25 - 22

Black
5 - 9

10

White
29 - 25

Black
1 - 5

11

White
21 x 14

Black
14 - 17

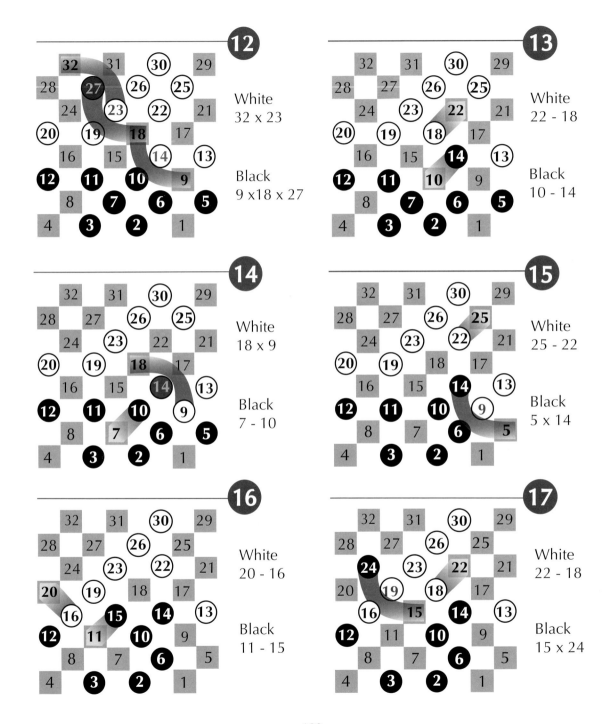

12

White
32 x 23

Black
9 x18 x 27

13

White
22 - 18

Black
10 - 14

14

White
18 x 9

Black
7 - 10

15

White
25 - 22

Black
5 x 14

16

White
20 - 16

Black
11 - 15

17

White
22 - 18

Black
15 x 24

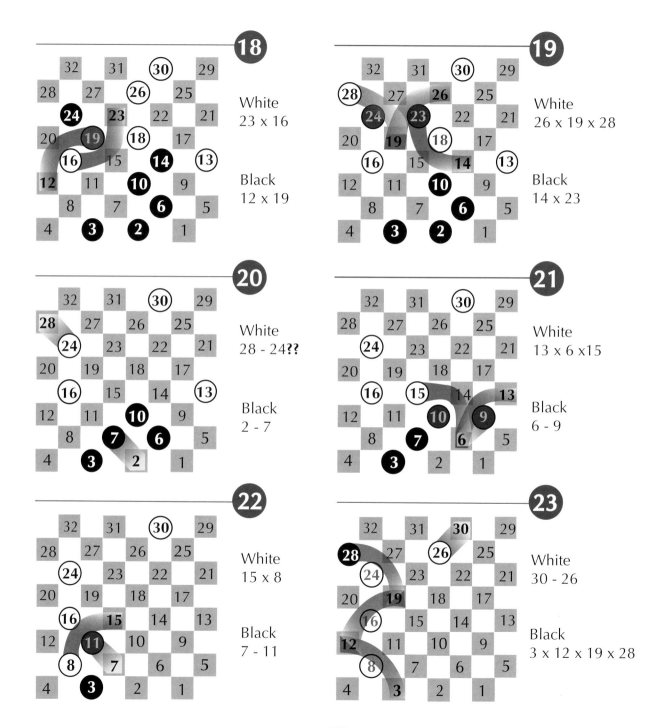

18

White
23 x 16

Black
12 x 19

19

White
26 x 19 x 28

Black
14 x 23

20

White
28 - 24??

Black
2 - 7

21

White
13 x 6 x15

Black
6 - 9

22

White
15 x 8

Black
7 - 11

23

White
30 - 26

Black
3 x 12 x 19 x 28

CITY GAME

Move	Black	White
1.	11-15	23-19
2.	8-11	22-17
3.	11-16	17-13
4.	16 x 23	26 x 19
5.	9-14	24-20
6.	15 x 24	28 x 19
7.	4-8	27-23
8.	8-11	31-26
9.	5-9	25-22
10.	1-5	29-25
11.	14-17	21 x 14
12.	9 x 27	32 x 23
13.	10-14	22-18
14.	7-10	18 x 9
15.	5 x 14	25-22
16.	11-15	20-16
17.	15 x 24	22-18
18.	12 x 19	23 x 16
19.	14 x 23	26 x 28
20.	2-7	28-24??
21.	6-9	13 x 15
22.	7-11	15 x 8
23.	3 x 28	30-26
24.	28-32K	

LEGEND

- *equals* Slide

x *equals* Jump

?? *equals* Move that lost the Game

K equals King Me. Crown Me!

CROWN ME!

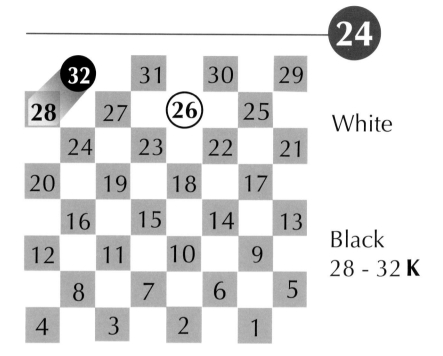

White

Black
28 - 32 **K**

Crown Me,
King Me,
Give that Sheriff a Gun,
Put a Stick in His Hand,
Put a Bone in His Mouth,
Put a Ring in His Nose,
Put a Hat On It!